1	The Green City
3	Bird Watching
6	A Walk with the Divine Farmer
10	Top 10 Scenes of West Lake
24	Solace in the Xixi Wetlands
28	The Bamboo-Lined Path at Yunqi
30	Qiantang River Tidal Bore
33	Hitting the Trails
34	The Pilgrim and the Hermit
36	The Maverick Monk
40	Pilgrims Praying for Sunny Days
42	The Southeastern Buddhist Kingdom
51	Looking for Immortals
54	Hangzhou Churches
57	Appendix

专业外教　英文朗读
扫码免费收听全书

更多英文原创中国故事
来《汉语世界》畅读
theworldofchinese.com

注册网站，点击右上角 subscribe 订阅，
输入优惠码 HANGZHOU
享受读者专属折扣！

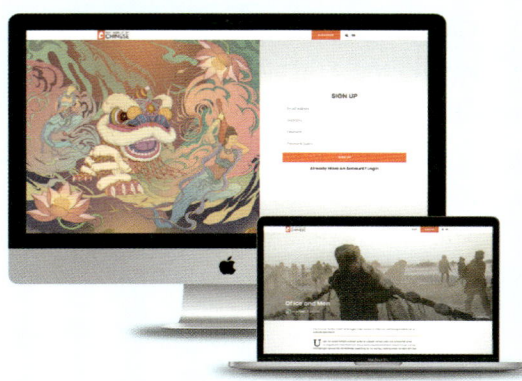

The Green City

The land, the waters, the climate—all played a role in creating the famous natural scenery of Hangzhou, but when it really comes down to it, Hangzhou's nature is a thousand-year-old dance between mankind and the wild. It may not have the peaks of Tibet or the biological diversity of Yunnan, but Hangzhou has a long history of humans and nature living side by side. From West Lake to the Qiantang River and from the Jade Emperor Hill to the Longjing Village, each bit of natural scenery in Hangzhou seems to tell a story of a land of civilization and a love of poetry and beauty.

One might think that the Xixi Wetlands have existed since the earth was young. In reality, seen from the sky, the wetlands appear as pools of green water carved to make way for sunshine. It wasn't the planet that made it this way, rather generations of rulers and literati who wanted to expand upon the area's natural beauty.

Today, the labors of the ancients can be seen in the cranes, egrets, and

peak
山峰

make way for
为……让路

literati
文人

egret
白鹭

杭州一瞥：云水禅心

kingfisher
翠鸟

blossom
花

mallard
绿头鸭

carp
鲤鱼

thrive
茁壮成长

kingfishers of the Xixi Wetlands, in the lotus and peach blossoms that dot and decorate nearly every step along West Lake, in the mallards and carp that thrive in the city's causeways and canals.

Bird Watching

While much of the biodiversity of the past has made way for skyscrapers and Hangzhou's numerous ancient architectural wonders, the city remains one of the most popular places in China for bird watching. Birders come from all around the world to see Hangzhou's birds.

Birders at the Lake

Normally, birders find themselves having to travel far outside the major cities to see the birds, but this is not the case with Hangzhou. West Lake's wide berth and central location makes the area a paradise for birders wanting to catch these creatures in flight with lotus flowers or plum blossoms, depending on the season.

Even here, in the heart of modernity, visitors can catch glimpses of the common kingfisher, the ashy drongo, the oriental magpie-robin, and black-throated tits. All of these birds come, like most of the visitors, for the peace of West Lake—but also the insects.

---

biodiversity
生物多样性

birder
观鸟者

berth
停泊处

glimpse
瞥见

ashy drongo
灰卷尾

oriental magpie-robin
鹊鸲

black-throated tit
红头长尾山雀

Mandarin duck
鸳鸯

fidelity
忠诚

prominent
重要的

waterfowl
水禽

be drawn to
被吸引

heron
苍鹭

China's Love Birds

Native to East Asia, the Mandarin duck has a special cultural importance in China as a symbol of love and fidelity. They are also the most prominent visitors to West Lake every year from late October to early April; during this time, up to 300 wild Mandarin ducks can be seen swimming and flying over the lake. The best spot to catch a glimpse of these birds is the West Lake Waterfowl Protection Zone west of the Su Causeway.

Wetland Waterfowl

Now, West Lake and Hangzhou Botanical Garden are all well and good, but, like most parts of Hangzhou, if you really want a taste of nature, you've got to head to the Xixi National Wetland Park. Here, birders from around the world try to catch glimpses of eastern China's colorful waterfowl in an environment that has mystical waterways and magic boatmen.

Besides all of the extremely active ducks in the area, birders will find themselves drawn to the herons that can be found throughout the area. Unlike the colorful birds one finds in the botanical garden, these herons are largely native and some can rise pretty high on the East China aviary food chain.

These wetland herons are sometimes overlooked in favor of the perhaps more strange-looking egrets, a favorite being the eastern cattle egret—notable for its perfectly white plumage out of breeding season.

However, chief among all of these bird watching experiences is finding the brown hawk-owl, perhaps the greatest hunter in all of East China. You can find them in the Xixi Wetlands using their almost supernatural owl-eyes and hawk-like body to hunt the small rodents inhabiting the shallow, brackish waters.

It is here, in the Xixi Wetlands, that the avian diversity of Hangzhou can truly be seen, even the most picky nature lover can find something special in the skies and branches of Hangzhou.

aviary
鸟类的

overlook
忽视

eastern cattle egret
牛背鹭

notable
引人注目的

plumage
全身羽毛

brown hawk-owl
褐鹰鸮

rodent
啮齿动物

inhabit
居住

brackish
微咸的

A Walk with the Divine Farmer

divine
神圣的

sage
圣人

beverage
饮料

come sb's way
被某人碰到

refreshing
清爽的

lush
茂盛的

slot
时间段

yield
生产

pre-Qingming Longjing
明前龙井

premium
最佳的

No one is absolutely sure about when the Chinese began to fall in love with tea. Most will tell you that a legendary sage some 4,500 years ago named Shennong, or Divine Farmer, discovered this magical beverage. It's said that he would march through the thick forests, studying every strange plant to come his way. By tasting them, he was able to identify their medicinal properties. Thus began humanity's long, long history of drinking tea. In the exploratory spirit of the Divine Farmer, there's no place more fitting for a hike through tea culture than Hangzhou's refreshing tea gardens.

Every spring, in late March, the lush tea gardens across the slopes in the West Lake region come alive. If you happen to visit during this time, you will find, under the straw hats that dot the green bushes, farmers working as quickly as possible to pick the tender tea leaves. They have a narrow time slot (two weeks or so) to yield the most precious green tea there is, called pre-Qingming Longjing. Once the Qingming Festival is past, the tea loses its premium status.

Named after a sweet local well called "Longjing," or "Dragon Well," (which you will also see along the trail), Longjing tea plants are what you will mainly encounter strolling among the tea gardens spreading on the hills near West Lake. Only tea from the West Lake region, a little over 168 square kilometers, can be named "West Lake Longjing." This tea is ranked first on China's finest tea selections. The fruit of a skilled tea picker's entire day only yields half a kilogram of ready tea after processing—made this bittersweet, fragrant tea a highly sought-after, though pricy, delight.

To start your journey, the China National Tea Museum, Shuangfeng Branch at Longjing Road serves as a nice first stop to gather all your tea facts.

A number of tempting tea houses can be found in the museum, but you can also head southwest into the village to try a pot. Nearly all the families are somehow involved in tea business, and visitors will be able to see tea-makers working in their front yards with frying pans full of tea leaves. Hangzhou locals love to take a whole day to relax here, immersed in the tea field surrounding village while tasting fresh tea.

trail
小径

stroll
漫步

West Lake Longjing
西湖龙井

fragrant
芳香的

immerse
沉浸

hand-picked 精选的	Head west on Longjing Road and you will pass the Eight Scenes of Longjing that are scattered in the valley, pavilion, temple, pond, spring—each hand-picked and named by Emperor Qianlong during his four visits to the Longjing area. One of the spots, Fenghuang Ridge, is covered with bamboo. It's also the steepest climb along the route.
ridge 山脊	
steep 陡峭的	
breeze 微风	Your next stop should be Longjing Temple for the surrounding lush tea fields and cool breeze far from the noise and commerce of the city. Most importantly, it's where the Longjing tea legend began, for the Dragon Well dwells inside. In the Northern Song Dynasty, the temple resembled a high society salon where the most talented literati of the day and highest ranking officials (often they were both) gathered to taste tea and chat. On a giant rock in the temple, you will find a fitting phrase for your tour, "龙井问茶," "investigating the secrets of tea through Longjing." This tour is also regarded as one of the New Top 10 Scenes of West Lake.
dwell 存在	
resemble 象征	
pit stop 中途停车点	

Past the Longjing Temple is Longjing Village, a great place for another pit stop to fill up your tea meter in the convenient tea house at the mountain foot of Shifeng Hill. Following along to the tea market, this is where you'll want to get out your wallet for tea that can't be found anywhere else. Longjing Village is one of the only places on earth where you'll have the opportunity to drink authentic Shifeng Longjing at a fair price. From here, you can either end the journey by walking down the Nine Brooks and Eighteen Streams all the way to the main road along the Qiantang River; or, you could choose to continue the journey to climb Shifeng Hill to find the Hugong Temple, which has a small tea garden of 18 stalks. But they were once directly owned by Emperor Qianlong, who picked their leaves and brought them back for his mother. Next, you could follow the trail called by locals "Shili-langdang Ridge" and head to your final destination, Meijiawu Village, the biggest natural village where the West Lake Longjing tea is produced. This peaceful village, with a history of 600 years, is the perfect place to rest your feet in the many tea houses.

stalk
株

Top 10 Scenes of West Lake

aesthetic
美学的

inspire
给予灵感

give rise to
产生了

rejuvenate
使复原

inscribe
刻

The Top 10 Scenes of West Lake are based on an age-old aesthetic tradition that dates back to the 12th century and has inspired some of the best literature and art in Chinese civilization. These scenes are artworks themselves, made by both humans and nature. The earliest reference to these 10 scenes appeared in the Southern Song Dynasty when the construction of the lake was at its peak. As the capital city, Lin'an, today known as Hangzhou, attracted talented scholars, writers, and artists, giving rise to many lake-themed *shanshui* or Chinese landscape paintings. With the fall of the Southern Song Dynasty, these scenes were forgotten, but they came back to the surface four centuries later when Emperor Kangxi of the Qing Dynasty took an interest and rejuvenated the lake with his works of calligraphy and poetic names. Today, you can find these names inscribed on a stele at their respective locations.

Spring Dawn at Su Causeway

Named after Song poet and Hangzhou governor Su Shi, this expansive causeway cuts through the western third of West Lake—a 2,800-meter belt perfect for biking. The reason spring is the best time to visit is evident in the peach blossoms as well as the soft willows. Perhaps the best way to enjoy the path is to start off at the north, a stone's throw from the Shangri-La Hotel. Walk, jog, or bike down the causeway to admire its six bridges and their charms.

Breeze Ruffled Lotus at Quyuan Garden

Quyuan Garden is well-known for its lotus, and in high summer you'll also see plenty of steam rising from the green surface of the pond. The garden used to be a brewery for making wine in the Southern Song Dynasty.

Autumn Moon over the Calm Lake

When late autumn comes and the moon is full, the scenery here is renowned for its romance. Located at Bai Causeway's western point on Gushan Hill, this spot is one of the best places for a panoramic view of the lake. Of course,

---

expansive
广阔的

willow
杨柳

a stone's throw
近在咫尺

ruffle
吹皱

brewery
酿酒厂

be renowned for
以……著称

panoramic
全景

杭州一瞥：云水禅心

cruise 乘船游览	
serenity 宁静	
linger 流连	
abuzz 热闹的	
snapshot 快照	
intact 完好无损的	
flake 雪花	
illusion 幻觉	
spectacular 惊人的	
swirl 漩涡	
nestle 坐落	

you can also jump on a boat, cruising while appreciating the serenity of the moonlit lake.

Lingering Snow on the Broken Bridge

When rare snow hits, this area is abuzz with visitors (particularly couples) looking for that perfect snapshot of the Broken Bridge. Located at the eastern end of the Bai Causeway in the north of the lake, the Broken Bridge, contrary to its name, is firm and intact. It only appears to be broken after a snowfall when the sunny side of the bridge melts the newly-fallen flakes. With its dark brown surface revealed, it creates an illusion that the bridge is broken from the Bai Causeway. But what really makes this site spectacular is its role in the famous folk tale "Legend of the White Snake"—as the spot where the couple in this romantic story first met—making it one of the most romantic spots in Hangzhou.

Viewing Fish at Flower Pond

Swirls of colorful carp make these ponds into living paintings. Nestled at the southern end of Su Causeway, the area was once owned by a few ancient officials and literati as a lakeside villa, and over time it has been decorated with gardens of rockeries and pavilions. The Red Fish Pond is located at the center of the garden. An interesting scene at this spot is when the brocade carps compete for fallen peach blossom petals in spring.

Orioles Singing in the Willows

This is where locals and visitors alike go to get away from it all: 200,000 square meters of beauty and willows. In spring, the songs of the orioles ring through the willows, mixed with elderly Hangzhou residents singing classical Chinese operas. The orioles in China aren't just favored for their songs; they're a symbol of vitality and the natural order.

Three Pools Mirroring the Moon

If you find yourself far from Hangzhou and still long for the Three Pools Mirroring the Moon, just take a one-yuan note from your pocket and look at the back. Obviously much better in person, this little islet features three two-meter-tall pagodas with an almost ethereal beauty. Marked with five round

---

brocade carp
锦鲤

petal
花瓣

oriole
莺

vitality
活力

islet
小岛

ethereal
空灵的

shimmering
闪烁微光的

pierce
刺入

poke
戳

holes, these pagodas are lit at night to match the shimmering shape of the full autumn moon. Booking a boat early is a necessity.

Twin Peaks Piercing the Clouds

The best viewing spot for the twin peaks is by the Hongchun Bridge in the northwestern corner of West Lake. If you're lucky enough to be visiting on a foggy day, you will see both peaks poking through the clouds during a morning stroll. About five kilometers apart, the Southern Peak is over 256 meters tall, about 100 meters shorter than the Northern Peak. A hike to the Northern Peak will take you through the Lingyin Temple scenic area.

Leifeng Pagoda in Evening Glow

The "glowing" reputation of this pagoda can be seen in the evening, when the color of imperial Buddhist red shines with the sunset. But, if you mention this site to anyone in China, the first thing to come to mind is the myth of the White Snake, who, legend has it, is still trapped beneath this pagoda.

Evening Bell Ringing at Nanping Hill

At first sight, this spot might not seem to have any particular importance, but just close your eyes and listen. Around 4 p.m. every day, the evening bell inside Jingci Temple on the northern slope of Nanping Hill resonates against the hills; the sound travels across the lake and echoes when it meets the stone of Geling Hill. Inside the Jingci Temple, people often ignite their incense sticks and pray. It's also customary for local people in Hangzhou to visit Jingci Temple on Chinese New Year's Eve to strike the bell in a spirit of respect and reflection.

resonate
共鸣

echo
回声

ignite
点燃

incense stick
香

杭州一瞥：云水禅心

Spring Dawn at Su Causeway

HANGZHOU HERMITS

杭州一瞥：云水禅心

Breeze Ruffled Lotus at Quyuan Garden

HANGZHOU HERMITS

杭州一瞥：云水禅心

Autumn Moon over the Calm Lake

HANGZHOU HERMITS

杭州一瞥：云水禅心

Lingering Snow on the Broken Bridge

HANGZHOU HERMITS

Solace in the Xixi Wetlands

solace
慰藉

downtown
市中心

inspiration
灵感

The Xixi National Wetland Park has been carefully protected to reflect a history of Hangzhou's "man and nature" dance. It is just a short cab ride from downtown. But, the real purpose of the wetlands is to preserve, protect, and guide the ancient natural beauty of Hangzhou. Today, just five kilometers from West Lake, nature lovers can wander over 11 square kilometers of the wetlands.

The Literati of the Lakes

It's difficult to talk about anywhere in Hangzhou without talking about poetry, and in the Xixi Wetlands the ancient poets and scholars lived in peaceful coexistence with nature, choosing them as a place of inspiration.

Foremost among the attractions of the poetry of the Xixi Wetlands is perhaps the Xixi Waterside Villas, considered even today as a site for great literary minds to meet. Nowadays, the site is mainly used as a sort of library of great works. More specifically, one might want to visit the Plum and Bamboo

Villa, built in the 18th century by literary man Zhang Cibai, where, you probably guessed, the highlight is the plum blossoms and bamboo. Traveling southeast from there, literature lovers will find the famous Xixi Thatched House, formerly home to Ming Dynasty scholar and poet Feng Mengzhen.

For the most famous spot for literary inspiration in the wetlands, you're going to need to take a boat. The Autumn Snow Temple is only accessible by water on a solitary islet in the center of the wetlands surrounded by thick reeds.

Birds and Natural Beauty

The natural beauty that inspired all those poets and scholars can still be found today. The first thing that comes to mind is that of the birds. While modernity may have chased out a number of predators that used to inhabit much of the area, the waterfowl and egrets of the area are simply terrific against a backdrop of idyllic scenery and Qing-era architecture.

The Xixi Wetlands boast 180 different species of birds and are an ideal spot for catching delightful glimpses of egrets,

---

highlight
亮点

thatched house
茅草屋

accessible
可到达的

solitary
偏僻的

reed
芦苇

predator
捕食者

backdrop
背景

idyllic
田园的

boast
以……著称

kestrel
茶隼

reptile
爬行动物

ecological
生态的

conservation
保护

kestrels, and kingfishers. Birds making their tireless journey from Siberia to Australia and back find solace in the calm waters, much to the enjoyment of birdwatchers all over the world who come to look for rare species in this heavenly setting.

And, while birds may be what the park is most famous for (along with a few reptiles), its biodiversity is most visible at the Underwater Ecological Observation Corridor where curious passers-by can observe some of the underwater creatures found in the wetlands.

Getting Around Paradise

With 11.5 square kilometers of wetlands under conservation, even the most avid hiker will need to admit that doing the whole of the Xixi Wetlands on foot is simply impossible. That said, there are a number of areas best seen walking at a slow pace, chief among which are the Green Causeway and the Blessed Causeway. The Green Causeway will take you by the Underwater Ecological Observation Corridor, but, more importantly, it takes you through the Hangzhou Wetland Botanical Garden, where fans of flowers are in for a treat. To hike the Green Causeway, enter via the east gate or Wensan West Road access point and follow the signs.

Going west, the Green Causeway meets the Blessed Causeway, and here you're going to need to make a choice. Head north to perhaps a more peaceful area, which includes the Jiangcun Village Leisure Life Block, to grab a bite to eat; or go straight ahead through Hezhu Street packed with shops and diners. South, however, is probably the best option; turn east at the end of causeway after a peaceful walk through the greenery, and you will find Gao's Villa. While a walk is certainly a welcome way to see the Xixi Wetlands, you're going to want a boat for the whole experience. Once you are on Hezhu Street, the closest dock is Shentankou; here's where the wetlands journey really begins. Board one of the electric boats for a leisurely guided cruise around some of the most amazing sites in the wetlands, including the thick reeds covering Autumn Snow Temple, Reflection of Red Persimmon in Water, and Plum and Bamboo Villa. There is no right way to see the Xixi Wetlands. It is an area of unmatched peace and quiet just a few kilometers from the city.

diner
食客

greenery
绿色植物

persimmon
柿子

The Bamboo-Lined Path at Yunqi

While you're enjoying the famous tea gardens of Hangzhou, you might find yourself in the relative peace of the Bamboo-lined Path at Yunqi. Bamboo, for some, is regarded as a model for a proper gentleman in traditional Chinese culture, representing uprightness, elegance, and simplicity. As you ascend, you might also notice the sound of a stream running nearby. The bamboo lining slowly gives way to tightly packed trees and greenery that give the area the feel of a crowded canopy forest.

For a true look at the long stretch of Hangzhou's proud forests, there is nowhere better than the bamboo-lined path. One often gets the impression in Chinese parks and sites that everything has been manicured, but the bamboo-lined path has been spared. This is where you can see some of the most beautiful trees in East China.

Take, for instance, the 330-year-old camphor tree about halfway up the path. The camphor is the official tree of Hangzhou. The rest of the path provides excellent information on trees that are even older—some more than 1,000 years old.

---

uprightness
正直

ascend
登高

give way to
让步

canopy
树荫

manicured
修剪整齐的

camphor tree
樟树

The main path is paved with cobblestones with a line running down the middle. It is said that, in the Qing Dynasty, the middle section was reserved for emperors Kangxi and Qianlong during their visits here, and anyone who stepped on it would be arrested, or even executed.

Under the shade of historic trees and walking the path of the emperors, visitors reach the top of the path for what many consider to be the most beautiful view in all of Hangzhou. While all seasons offer great scenery atop this mile-long hike, "*yunqi*" means lingering clouds, so the best time to see it might be when fog is rushing over the tea fields.

cobblestone
鹅卵石

execute
处死

Qiantang River Tidal Bore

tidal bore
潮涌

affectionate
关爱的

prospect
展望

Qiantang River is a changeable mother to the people that live by her side. She is gentle and affectionate most of the time, but her dark mood changes have caused serious destruction.

Located on the lower reaches of the largest river in Zhejiang Province, Qiantang River runs through the central districts of Hangzhou from the southwest to the northeast. On its north is the city's cultural and historical center spreading to the eastern side of West Lake, the land that once held the capitals of the ancient Wuyue Kingdom and the glorious Southern Song Dynasty. The southern bank holds the city's urban future—prospected by both the city government and private developers.

If you trace the river upstream to the west, you will encounter its middle and upper sections, Fuchun River and Xin'an River. This road that trips through the Hangzhou-Qiandao Express Highway offers a refreshing experience that will throw you into the beauty of the green mountains and gentle rivers along the way, eventually leading to the lake resort paradise, Qiandao Lake, or

"Thousand-isle Lake." Downstream, the Qiantang River runs into the East China Sea at Hangzhou Bay—a bell-shaped bay that opens up dramatically from a few kilometers to 100 kilometers. The unique shape of the river's mouth, combined with tidal forces, created the world's largest river tidal bore, where the difference between high and low tides can be as much as ten meters. Though it appears every month, the best time to view the biggest tidal bore is around August 18 on the Chinese traditional calendar, which is around mid-September.

The best location to view the tidal bore is in Yanguan Town, roughly 50 kilometers on the northeast of Hangzhou. But closer to home in Xiaoshan District, you can also find a tidal bore viewing area at Qiantang River Tidal Bore Watching Resort.

unique
独一无二的

Liuhe Pagoda

tame
驯服

beacon
灯塔

ruin
毁坏

compromise
使……陷入危险

The Liuhe Pagoda, or "The Pagoda of Six Harmonies," is a giant, wooden, seven-story pagoda that you can actually climb. Spacious corridors on each level and big windows open to all directions make this a great spot to view the natural scenery, most impressively the Qiantang River. First built in the 10th century with the belief that it could tame the tidal bore, it was also a beacon for boats cruising the Qiantang River at night.

Though it is a special example of nature's power, the tidal bore also endangers the people along the river. Once flooded, it not only takes lives and destroys property, but the salty sea water can also ruin farmland for years.

Countless years were spent building river dams here throughout history. In the Qing Dynasty, Emperor Qianlong visited Hangzhou six times. Each time he inspected the Qiantang River dams, which were of national importance.

Today's modern architecture helps to control the tidal bore, but in recent years, there's still occasional news of a tourist's safety being compromised. So while appreciating the view, be sure to remember nature's cruel side and stay safe.

Hitting the Trails

Hangzhou's southwestern mountains are a treasure for those who enjoy idyllic walks. The height of most of the mountains ranges between 200 to 300 meters, so you are unlikely to suffer a tiring, steep climb for longer than an hour.

The mountains are at their best after a rainy day. The damp forests display a particularly rich green and smell sweeter, and you keep going in and out of floating mists as you climb higher. However, the paths do not have protective measures in place, so do watch out for the slippery moss on the stone pavements and wear outdoor shoes. You should also bring some food and water.

This route takes about five hours, and presents you with the large variety of landscapes that Hangzhou has to offer. The part from the Bamboo-lined Path at Yunqi to Zhenji Temple is a 50-minute constant climb, but once it's over, you can finish the rest at a leisurely pace.

moss
苔藓

pavement
石板路

The Pilgrim and the Hermit

pilgrim
香客

hermit
隐士

monastery
僧院

incense
香

environmentally-friendly
环保的

Buddhist monasteries have a tradition of taking over the most scenic mountains, which makes paying them a visit a must if you want to appreciate Hangzhou from the clouds. You can wander in the vast mountains to the southwest of West Lake following the ancient paths through forests once traveled by hermits; or, you can pretend to be a devotional pilgrim, offering incense and praying for health and fortune in the famous temples of Tianzhu and Lingyin.

The local government's care for these sites ensures a good monastery experience. Tourists are given three pieces of environmentally-friendly incense for free upon entrance, but you're not allowed to bring your own due to the effects that they can have on the environment.

However, as safe and peaceful as a day in the mountains can be, there are a few things you're going to need to remember: ladies should wear pants, not skirts; do not walk in between a praying person and the Buddha to which they are praying; in most cases, Buddhist monks do not want you to photograph the statues in prayer halls, but you can try to ask for permission if you want; and, above all, do not waste food if you dine in a monastery.

The Maverick Monk

maverick
特立独行的

swig
牛饮

excessive
过度的

venerable
令人尊重的

teetotaler
禁酒主义者

contemplation
沉思

sutra reading
诵经

abbot
住持

mixed bag
毁誉参半

sinful
有罪的

"I only wish that West Lake was filled with wine. Then I would lie by its side with my gown loose, taking a swig whenever a wave swept upon me." While most ancient Chinese poets were indeed known for their excessive drinking, this poem stands out because it was written by a Buddhist monk called the Venerable Daoji who, it goes without saying, was supposed to be a teetotaler. Besides the bottle, Daoji also enjoyed meat and the company of women—as much as his wallet would allow. He believed that monks were as blind in the mind as donkeys and that contemplation and sutra reading only serve to make one lifeless.

Daoji lived his wildest days in Hangzhou; he died and was buried in the city. The abbots of two major Hangzhou monasteries, Lingyin Temple and Jingci Temple, saw the wisdom behind his madness and treated him with respect for much of his life. Daoji's fame was, one might say, a mixed bag. Apart from his sinful deeds, Daoji was known among those who knew him as a generous friend, a warm-hearted character, and a philosopher who lived his faith, as well as a refined poet and calligrapher.

In Ming and Qing novels, he was depicted as possessing supernatural powers, the savior of the unfortunate, and a punisher of evil. Remembered by the nickname "Jigong," he remains a favorite monk in the minds of the Chinese people, and his legend is still passed on in novels and TV shows today. In many Chinese monasteries, Daoji is worshiped as a deity, a skinny monk in a tall, pointed hat and torn robes, standing (with difficulty) while holding a cracked fan and, of course, a pot of wine, receiving worship and prayer with a permanent ironic smile.

You can pay homage to Daoji in Lingyin Temple, where there is Jigong Hall with frescos telling his tales. The fresco, although painted in 2011, was done in an elegant Southern Song Dynasty style by artist Lin Haizhong, and it's worth the time it takes to go and see it.

You can see more of Daoji in Hupao Park, where he was buried and enshrined.

---

calligrapher
书法家

depict
描写

savior
救星

worship
崇拜

deity
神

cracked
破裂的

homage
敬意

fresco
壁画

enshrine
供奉

Hupao Park

Although now known as "Hupao Park," for over a thousand years, the area was a Chan monastery. Dating back to the end of the Tang Dynasty in the beginning of the ninth century, the monastery began as a mere hut built by a monk called Chan Master Huanzhong, destroyed and rebuilt many times over the past one thousand years. On entering Hupao Park, it's easy to see why Chan monks found it so pleasant; it is built along a mountain slope, well-shaded by tall, arched trees with the famous Hupao Spring running through. With the coming of spring, the vegetation here is particularly varied. Although today the former monastery has been turned into several exhibition halls, a walk through the park is itself a Zen-like experience. Going up you will find Jigong Hall and Jigong Stupa, the great man's tomb.

The neighboring Jigong Hall is the Memorial Hall for Li Shutong and his stupa. Li Shutong, also known as the Venerable Master Hongyi, was an artist and Buddhist scholar in whom Hangzhou takes particular pride. He was also an accomplished musician, poet,

---

arched
拱形的

vegetation
植被

Zen
禅宗的

stupa
佛塔

accomplished
技艺高超的

calligrapher, seal engraver, and painter—
as well as one of the earliest pioneers
of modern Chinese theater. In 1918,
Li officially converted to monkhood in
Hupao Temple and got the name Hongyi
at the age of 39. In his later years, he
became an established scholar in the
Vinaya School and brought about the
sect's last revival in China.

seal engraver
篆刻家

convert to monkhood
出家

Vinaya School
律宗

sect
宗派

revival
复兴

Pilgrims Praying for Sunny Days

Hangzhou rain, gentle as it is, is a constant, patient drizzle that gradually soaks you and even your bed sheets can feel damp with the constant spritz. Take Monk Zhinan's famous verse, for example, describing typical southern rain: "Under apricot blossoms the rain hardly wets your clothes, and by willow trees the wind is mild on your face." Despite the apricot and willow and the charming mist on West Lake, you will be yearning for a clear day and dry shoes.

This is why while pilgrims elsewhere may have prayed for money, those in Hangzhou prayed for sunny days. If you feel too troubled by the continuous Hangzhou rain, do what the locals have done since the Song Dynasty: go to Shangtianzhu Temple and pray for a sunny day.

The Three Temples at Tianzhu

There are three monasteries on Tianzhu Road: Shangtianzhu, Zhongtianzhu, and Xiatianzhu.

Shangtianzhu, also named Faxi Monastery, is the largest of the three. It was rebuilt in the 1980s, but in its yard there

---

spritz
细雨

verse
诗句

apricot blossom
杏花

mist
薄雾

yearn for
渴望

are magnolia trees and bamboo stalks that are over 500 years old. Its dining hall offers decent vegetarian lunch from 11:00 a.m. to 12:30 a.m. with an entrance fee of 10 RMB, and lunch runs to about 5 RMB. When you dine in a monastery, you are required to stay quiet throughout the lunch and not to waste food.

Zhongtianzhu is also named Fajing Monastery, about one kilometer away from Shangtianzhu, and it's free to all. If you turn into the quiet, empty path to its north called Zhongfa Road, you will walk past Hangzhou's first famous boutique hotel, Amanfayun, which is based on the renovation of an century-old tea village, following on, the path leads to the Hangzhou Buddhist Academy. Both the hotel and the college are a nice combination of modern and traditional styles with pleasant stops for a scenic walk. If you turn left when you arrive at the fork at the end of the road, you will be heading to Lingyin Temple about 1.5 kilometers away.

Xiatianzhu, also named Fajing Nunnery, is only half a kilometer from Zhongtianzhu. It is the only nunnery in Hangzhou. Dating back to 330 BCE, it is the most ancient temple on Tianzhu Hill, with its major prayer halls built in the late Qing Dynasty. Admittance is 10 RMB.

magnolia
木兰花

boutique hotel
精品酒店

renovation
翻修

fork
岔路

nunnery
尼姑庵

The Southeastern Buddhist Kingdom

suppression
镇压

persecution
迫害

resume secular lifestyle
还俗

doom
厄运

regime
政权

Toward the end of the Tang Dynasty, in 842, Emperor Wuzong started a nationwide suppression on Buddhist monasteries and monks, which is the largest Buddhist persecution in China's ancient history. Over the next five years, over 4,600 monasteries were destroyed and 260,000 Buddhist monks and nuns were forced to resume secular lifestyles, causing Buddhism to lose its overwhelming position in Chinese culture, never to be regained to quite the same extent.

The suppression spread all the way to the south, and even the Lingyin Temple, one of Hangzhou's earliest and biggest monasteries, wasn't an exception.

As Buddhism went into its downfall, the powerful Tang Dynasty was also facing its doom and was soon divided into many kingdoms. Lingyin and other monasteries in Hangzhou were largely destroyed until in 907, when a new regime, the Wuyue Kingdom, ruled the area. The Wuyue Kingdom was relatively small—covering only today's

Zhejiang Province and part of Jiangsu and Fujian—but during the 72 years of its reign, it brought peace and prosperity to the land. Its rulers, also, were all devoted to the revival of Buddhism. Hundreds of monasteries were built in the mountains surrounding West Lake, and the kingdom attracted the top intellectual monks who found it a refuge from the social unrest and wars in the north. The kingdom is remembered as the "Southeastern Buddhist Kingdom," a name still in use to refer to the area.

The Wuyue Kingdom's first ruler, Qian Liu, invited a nationally-renowned monk, Venerable Master Yanshou, to rebuild Lingyin. Under constant expansion, by the mid-10th century, Lingyin again became one of the most magnificent monasteries in southern China, with 72 prayer halls and over 1,300 rooms housing over 3,000 monks. Venerable Yanshou also supervised the construction of the giant Liuhe Pagoda, which was built to bring under control the flood-bringing dragon in the Qiantang River.

During the Southeastern Buddhist Kingdom period, some significant changes happened in Buddhism and those changes endure even today. The

reign
当政

refuge
避难所

unrest
动乱

endure
持续

Pure Land practice
净土宗

champion
捍卫者

secularization
世俗化

icon
偶像

Pure Land practice—a simplified way of practicing Buddhism that emphasized religious devotion over philosophical thinking, with Venerable Yanshou as one of its key champions—gradually grew into a trend. By the Song Dynasty, Pure Land societies had already become popular across the country. In the Tang Dynasty, Chinese Buddhism had been scholarly and philosophical, but with the popularized Pure Land practice, Buddhism took a big turn toward secularization, accessible for all, regardless of their class and education, and brought spiritual solace to scholars, officials, and ordinary people alike. New idols were created catering to the religious imagination of the masses, such as the merciful Guanyin and the fat, merry Maitreya Buddha, both becoming popular Chinese cultural icons.

Jingci Temple

Located opposite the Leifeng Pagoda, Jingci Temple was first built in 954 by King Qian Chu for Venerable Yanshou, where he was an abbot for 15 years. In the Song Dynasty, Jingci Temple played an important role in Buddhism's spreading from China to Korea and

Japan, and it is considered as the origin of the Caodong sect of Japanese Buddhism. It is also where Venerable Daoji spent his last years.

Caodong sect
曹洞宗

Statues on Feilai Peak

After you enter the Lingyin tourist area, you will find a series of Buddhist statues on Feilai Peak. Feilai, or Peak Flying from Afar, is a limestone cliff with a height of a mere 209 meters, but there are 334 preserved statues visible from there. The earliest statue was carved in 951, but 222 of the statues are from the Song Dynasty, including the famous Maitreya Buddha with the large cloth bag on the cliff to the southern bank of Lengquan Brook. The Maitreya Buddha was in fact a real historical figure called the "Cloth Bag Monk" from the ninth century, who was known for collecting unwanted food with a cloth bag. After his death people believed he was the reincarnation of the Maitreya Buddha, and to this day, among Han Chinese, the Maitreya Buddha is still in the image of the Cloth Bag Monk with a broad smile and a fat belly. There are 96 statues from the Yuan Dynasty or in the Yuan Dynasty style. The Yuan Mongol royals

limestone cliff
石灰岩悬崖

reincarnation
转世化身

> convert to
> 皈依
>
> relic
> 遗骨

converted to Tibetan Buddhism, so with these statues you can see a combination of the Tibetan and Han Buddhist sculpture styles.

Lingyin Temple

The Lingyin Temple was first built in 326 by an Indian monk called Chan Master Huili. Huili's relics are buried in the Ligong Pagoda by Feilai Peak, which dates back to 1547.

Ever since the Wuyue Kingdom, the Lingyin Temple has always been known for its magnificence and its association with the royal court, high-rank monks, and intellectuals. In the Southern Song Dynasty it was listed as one of the five royal Chan monasteries, and in the Ming Dynasty it owned over 2,100 acres of farmland that extends all the way to today's Jiaxing City. In its nearly 1,700 years of history, the Lingyin Temple was brought to ruin many times by war, fire, and the wear and tear of time. However, again and again, it has managed to recover its old glory.

Today, Lingyin is the monastery with the most historical relics in Hangzhou and, compared with most Hangzhou monasteries, it's well-preserved. Its oldest relics are two stone pillars dating back to 969, one at the entrance and one at the exit, and two stone pagodas dating back to 960 in front of its major prayer hall, standing as proof to the monastery's heyday. Visitors need to pay another 30 RMB to enter the Lingyin Temple.

You may want to avoid visiting on Buddhist festivals, holidays, and weekends, because Lingyin, with its fame, is crowded with tourists and pilgrims. On these special occasions, you really need to prepare for a battle to go in there.

Yongfu Temple

If you find Lingyin too busy, just walk ahead for 200 meters and you will arrive at the gate of Yongfu Temple. For those who prefer peace and quiet, Yongfu Temple is an ideal destination. It's hard to figure out how a monastery that is so scenic and peaceful could have so few visitors. The Yongfu Temple comprises five separate courtyards built along the hillside, which used to belong to two monasteries. The first monastery was built by the Indian monk Huili around

---

pillar
经幢

heyday
最繁荣的时期

guqin
古琴

seal engraving
篆刻

362, and the second one was built around the mid-fifth century.

One of the most well-known monks from the Yongfu Temple is Venerable Xinyue, a Chan monk of the Caodong sect. He was one of the most famous *guqin* musicians in the Ming Dynasty, and stood out in seal engraving, calligraphy, and painting. He went to Japan in 1676 in response to a Japanese abbot's invitation and stayed in the country until his death. Not only did he take with him the teachings of the Caodong sect, he also spread seal art and refreshed the then-dying *guqin* tradition, thereafter known as the father of seal art and modern *guqin* in Japan.

Although the present monastery was rebuilt in 2003, the well-designed gardens and courtyards look ancient, as wild vines and moss cover the bright yellow walls and gardens, thickly paved with fallen leaves. The calligraphy inscribed on steles and boards are also a pleasure to see. The Fuquan Teahouse offers vegetarian lunch and Longjing tea boiled with the water from the mountain spring. The Yongfu Temple is free to enter, but the tea house costs 60 to 70 RMB per person.

Taoguang Temple

The path from Yongfu Temple to Taoguang Temple is a long, winding, laborious climb, but it's worth the sweat to get to this modest monastery on the hill. Unlike Lingyin and Yongfu's royal yellow walls, Taoguang features grey tiles, white walls, and red pillars, giving it a classic Chinese garden look. It is named after the Chan Master Taoguang, a poet monk who lived as a hermit here from 821 to 824. Many poets have dedicated their works to Taoguang Temple, although the monastery's most ardent believer seems to have been Emperor Qianlong of the Qing Dynasty, who wrote over a dozen poems praising its view and the solitary, Zen surroundings. At the top of the monastery you can enjoy a scenic view of Lingyin Hill, West Lake, and the Qiantang River.

It takes about half an hour to walk from Yongfu Temple to Taoguang Temple, which is free to enter.

---

winding
蜿蜒的

laborious
费力的

grey tile
青砖

ardent
热烈的

Lingyin Temple

Looking for Immortals

Who hasn't daydreamed about immortality?

Arguably, it's the Chinese Daoists who made the most significant attempts to achieve it. They experimented with alchemy and took pills that were supposed to fight against the process of dying; trained themselves with *qigong*, meditation, and fasting; studied how yin and yang worked, both in the universe and in their own bodies; and explored the final wisdom of wu wei (inaction).

For us ordinary people, Jade Emperor Hill is the place closest to such a Daoist heaven. The whole mountain is full of mysterious, Daoist designs. The road swirls up the mountain like coiled incense, while under the foot of the mountain is a field in the shape of the Daoist eight trigrams. Mists float about in the woods, especially on rainy days, sometimes so thick that you might lose your partner if you're not careful. The forest looks ancient and is growing in a wild manner; the stone path is often blocked by unbelievably thick vines over 100 years old, coming out of nowhere and disappearing into the woods downhill.

---

immortal
永生

arguably
按理说

alchemy
炼金术

meditation
冥思

fasting
禁食

wu wei
无为

coiled incense
盘香

eight trigrams
八卦

divine
占卜

Big Dipper
北斗七星

descend
下降

steam up
布满水汽

The Jade Emperor Hill first became renowned for its mysterious powers around 1725. At that time Li Wei, the governor of Zhejiang Province, was troubled by constant fires throughout Hangzhou. After the divining of feng shui, he put seven iron water tanks in Fuxing Temple, the Daoist temple on the top of Jade Emperor Hill, to overpower the fierce fire dragon. The tanks were known as "Big Dipper Tanks," as they were laid out in the shape of the Big Dipper. Today, there is a copy of the tanks above Zilai Cave.

Hangzhou people still practice the tradition of visiting Jade Emperor Hill on the eighth day of the Chinese Lunar New Year. It's the day when people should pray to the Jade Emperor, the highest power in the Daoist deity system, for his blessings in the coming year. But other than a few traditional festivals when the Jade Emperor is specially remembered, most of the time he is quiet and forgotten.

Zilai Cave

The name of Zilai Cave, literally "The cave where purple clouds descend," indicates a very lucky sign in Daoism. It may be accurate; on sunny days, the cave does steam up. The small gate leads to three large caves inside with shrines of Daoist deities. It's dark, damp, and cold inside, and it takes a bit of an adventurous spirit to visit all three caves, but they are a good place to cool yourself off in summer.

Fuxing Temple

The Fuxing Temple stands at the top of Jade Emperor Hill. It's said to have been built around the beginning of the eighth century, but after a lot of reconstruction, it's now a simple temple surrounded by thick bamboo woods and mountain fog. The top is known as "Flying Clouds over Jade Emperor Hill" and is one of the most important sites of natural beauty in Hangzhou.

Baopu Daoist Temple

Baopu Daoist Temple is a sacred place for the Quanzhen School of Daoism. It is named after the book of alchemy and sorcery ***Baopuzi*** by the famous Daoist Ge Hong from the Eastern Jin Dynasty (317–420), who was said to have practiced alchemy here. The temple is located on Geling Hill to the north of West Lake behind Beishan Road. From the temple you can walk to Baoshi Hill.

---

shrine
圣坛

Quanzhen School of Daoism
全真教

sorcery
法术

Hangzhou Churches

immaculate
纯洁的

cathedral
大教堂

spill over into
鱼贯而入

missionary
传教士

Churchgoers visiting Hangzhou have a number of choices for services. Our Lady of the Immaculate Conception, known to locals simply as the "Catholic Church," lies on Zhongshan Northern Road in the downtown area. Built in 1661, it is one of the oldest cathedrals in China. Visitors should be warned, though, that during services on Sunday mornings, the cathedral quickly fills up and the crowd spills over into the car park area and toward the front gate.

Just around the corner you can find the Hangzhou Tianshui Church, which stands, appropriately enough, on Yesutang Alley or "The Church of Jesus Alley." Dating back to 1874, it is also a piece of Hangzhou history, where services tend to be in Mandarin.

Visitors can also choose to go to the Chong-yi Church on Xintang Road, Jianggan District. First established in 1866 by British missionary James Hudson Taylor, the church's new site was built in 2005 and covers an area of 12,480 square meters with a capacity for 5,500 people. It is considered the largest

Chinese church in the world.

Hangzhou Sicheng Christian Church on Jiefang Road, on the other hand, is the oldest Christian church in Hangzhou with a history of 96 years. The building is a combination of Western and Chinese style brick-wood architecture.

For English services, the Hangzhou International Christian Fellowship, or Gulou Tang (Drum Tower Church), is the best choice for visitors. Located near the Drum Tower and the tourist district of Qinghefang, it is well-situated for wandering around town once the service is over.

Hangzhou Phoenix Mosque

mosque
清真寺

Moroccan Sufi
伊斯兰教苏非派

minaret
宣礼塔

Known as one of the four greatest mosques in Southeast China, the Hangzhou Phoenix Mosque was built during the Tang Dynasty. It is a symbolic religious structure with more than a thousand years of history, marked with wonderful Arabic calligraphy and said to be built by an Egyptian trader. The mosque was once destroyed during the Song Dynasty but was rebuilt in 1281 and expanded to its current handsome form between 1451 and 1493. It once entertained the famous Moroccan Sufi traveler Ibn Battuta in the 1340s. Today the minarets and halls have been restored to their former splendor. Located on Zhongshan Middle Road, the same place it was more than a thousand years ago, the mosque is now over 2,600 square meters with a grand entrance hall and prayer area, still a functioning site of worship today.

Appendix

Place Names 地名机构名对照表

Amanfayun 法云安缦

Autumn Snow Temple 秋雪庵

Bai Causeway 白堤

Bamboo-lined Path at Yunqi 云栖竹径

Baopu Daoist Temple 抱朴道院

Baoshi Hill 宝石山

Big Dipper Tanks 七星缸

Blessed Causeway 福堤

Broken Bridge 断桥

Catholic Church 天主教堂

China National Tea Museum, Shuangfeng Branch 中国茶叶博物馆双峰馆区

Chong-yi Church 崇一堂

East China Sea 东海

Eight Scenes of Longjing 龙井八景

Memorial Hall for Li Shutong 李叔同纪念馆

Feilai Peak 飞来峰

Fenghuang Ridge 风篁岭

Fuchun River 富春江

Fuquan Teahouse 福泉茶院

Fuxing Temple 福星观

Gao's Villa 高庄

Geling Hill 葛岭

Green Causeway 绿堤

Gulou Tang (Hangzhou International Christian Fellowship) 鼓楼堂

Gushan Hill 孤山

Hangzhou Bay 杭州湾

Hangzhou Botanical Garden 杭州植物园

Hangzhou Buddhist Academy 杭州佛学院

Hangzhou Tianshui Church 天水堂

Hangzhou Wetland Botanical Garden 杭州湿地植物园

Hongchun Bridge 洪春桥

Hugong Temple 胡公庙

Hupao Park 虎跑公园

Hupao Spring 虎跑泉

Hupao Temple 虎跑寺

Jade Emperor Hill 玉皇山

Jiangcun Village Leisure Life Block 蒋村 (集市) 慢生活街区

Jianggan District 江干区

Jiaxing City 嘉兴市

Jigong Hall 济公殿

Jigong Stupa 济公塔院

Jingci Temple 净慈禅寺

Leifeng Pagoda 雷峰塔

Lengquan Brook 冷泉

Ligong Pagoda 理公塔

Lin'an 临安

Lingyin Hill 灵隐山

Lingyin Temple 灵隐寺

Liuhe Pagoda 六和塔

Longjing (Dragon Well) 龙井

Longjing Temple 龙井寺

Longjing Village 龙井村

Meijiawu Village 梅家坞村

Nanping Hill 南屏山

Nine Brooks and Eighteen Streams 九溪十八涧

Phoenix Mosque 凤凰寺

Plum and Bamboo Villa 梅竹山庄

Qiandao Lake 千岛湖

Qiantang River 钱塘江

Qiantang River Tidal Bore Watching Resort 钱江观潮城

Red Fish Pond 红鱼池

Shangri-La Hotel 香格里拉酒店

Shangtianzhu Temple (Faxi Monastery) 上天竺寺（法喜讲寺）

Shentankou Dock 深潭口码头

Shifeng Hill 狮峰山

Shili-langdang Ridge 十里琅珰

Siberia 西伯利亚

Sicheng Christian Church 思澄堂

Southeastern Buddhist Kingdom 东南佛国

Su Causeway 苏堤

Taoguang Temple 韬光寺

Tianzhu Hill 天竺山

Tibet 西藏

Underwater Ecological Observation Corridor 水下生态观光长廊

West Lake 西湖

West Lake Waterfowl Protection Zone 西湖水鸟保护区

Wuyue Kingdom 吴越国

Xiaoshan District 萧山区

Xiatianzhu Temple (Fajing Nunnery) 下天竺寺（法镜寺）

Xin'an River 新安江

Xixi National Wetland Park (Xixi Wetlands) 西溪国家湿地公园（西溪湿地）

Xixi Thatched House 西溪草堂

Xixi Waterside Villas 西溪水阁

Yanguan Town 盐官镇

Yongfu Temple 永福禅寺

Zhenji Temple 真迹寺

Zhongtianzhu Temple (Fajing Monastery) 中天竺寺（法净禅寺）

Zilai Cave 紫来洞

Names of Important Figures 人名对照表

Chan Master Huanzhong 寰中禅师

Chan Master Huili 慧理禅师

Chan Master Taoguang 韬光禅师

Cloth Bag Monk 布袋和尚

Emperor Kangxi 康熙皇帝

Emperor Qianlong 乾隆皇帝

Emperor Wuzong of Tang 唐武宗

Feng Mengzhen 冯梦祯

Ge Hong 葛洪

Guanyin 观音

Ibn Battuta 伊本·白图泰

Li Shutong 李叔同

Li Wei 李卫

Lin Haizhong 林海钟

Maitreya Buddha 弥勒佛

Monk Zhinan 僧人志南

Qian Chu 钱俶

Qian Liu 钱镠

Shennong 神农

Su Shi 苏轼

Venerable Daoji (Jigong) 道济法师 (济公)

Venerable Master Hongyi 弘一大师

Venerable Master Yanshou 延寿大师

Venerable Xinyue 东皋心越

Zhang Cibai 章次白

Top 10 Scenes of West Lake 西湖十景对照表

Autumn Moon over the Calm Lake
平湖秋月

Breeze Ruffled Lotus at Quyuan Garden 曲院风荷

Evening Bell Ringing at Nanping Hill
南屏晚钟

Leifeng Pagoda in Evening Glow
雷峰夕照

Lingering Snow on the Broken Bridge
断桥残雪

Orioles Singing in the Willows
柳浪闻莺

Spring Dawn at Su Causeway
苏堤春晓

Three Pools Mirroring the Moon
三潭印月

Twin Peaks Piercing the Clouds
双峰插云

Viewing Fish at Flower Pond
花港观鱼

Others 其他

Baopuzi, Book of the Master Who Embraces Simplicity 《抱朴子》

Flying Clouds over Jade Emperor Hill
玉皇飞云

Reflection of Red Persimmon in Water
火柿映波

图书在版编目 (CIP) 数据

杭州一瞥：精编版. 云水禅心：英文
蒋景阳主编；蒋景阳，李晓红编. —北京：商务印书馆，2023

ISBN 978-7-100-22540-3

Ⅰ. ①杭… Ⅱ. ①蒋… ②蒋… ③李… Ⅲ. ①英语—语言读物 ②旅游指南—杭州—英文 Ⅳ. ①H319.4：K

中国国家版本馆CIP数据核字(2023)第102975号

权利保留，侵权必究。

杭州一瞥：精编版

蒋景阳 主编

商 务 印 书 馆 出 版
（北京王府井大街36号 邮政编码100710）
商 务 印 书 馆 发 行
北京博海升彩色印刷有限公司印刷
ISBN 978-7-100-22540-3

2023 年 7 月第 1 版	开本 889×1194 1/32
2023 年 7 月第 1 次印刷	印张 7

定价：98.00 元